FIRE OUTDOORS

Fireplaces, Fire Pits, Wood Fired Ovens & Cook Centers

Tina Skinner & Melissa Cardona

Schiffer Publishing Ltd

4880 Lower Valley Road, Atglen, PA 19310 USA

Acknowledgments

Many thanks to Nathaniel Wolfgang-Price for his significant contribution to the production of this book.

Other Schiffer Books by Tina Skinner & Melissa Cardona

Fire Outdoors: Fireplaces, Fire Pits & Cook Centers
Creative Patios
Pools, Patios, and Fabulous Outdoor Living Spaces: Luxury by Master Pool Builders
Master Built Pools & Patios: An Inspiring Portfoio of Design Ideas
Hot Tubs & Spas: An Inspirational Design Guide
Pure Deck-adence
All Decked Out...Redwood Decks: Ideas and Plans for Contemporary Outdoor Living
The Deck Book: Inspirational Design Ideas
Paver Projects: Designs For Amazing Outdoor Environments
Retaining Walls

Other Schiffer Books on Related Subjects

Petite Patios & Intimate Garden Spaces
The Patio Portfolio: An Inspirational Design Guide
Patios, Driveways, and Plazas: The Pattern Language of Concrete Pavers
Backyards & Boulevards: A Portfolio of Concrete Paver Projects

Type set in Souvenir Lt BT/New Baskerville BT

ISBN: 0-7643-2397-0
Printed in China

Published by Schiffer Publishing Ltd.
4880 Lower Valley Road
Atglen, PA 19310
Phone: (610) 593-1777; Fax: (610) 593-2002
E-mail: Info@schifferbooks.com

For the largest selection of fine reference books on this and related subjects, please visit our web site at
www.schifferbooks.com
We are always looking for people to write books on new and related subjects. If you have an idea for a book please contact us at the above address.

This book may be purchased from the publisher.
Include $3.95 for shipping.
Please try your bookstore first.
You may write for a free catalog.

In Europe, Schiffer books are distributed by
Bushwood Books
6 Marksbury Ave.
Kew Gardens
Surrey TW9 4JF England
Phone: 44 (0) 20 8392-8585; Fax: 44 (0) 20 8392-9876
E-mail: info@bushwoodbooks.co.uk
Website: www.bushwoodbooks.co.uk
Free postage in the U.K., Europe; air mail at cost.

CONTENTS

INTRODUCTION

The introduction of fire into your outdoor living space defines it as a destination. Whether used for cooking, heating, or unveiling the night with light, the attraction of fire is undeniable. Thanks to clever manufacturers, designers, and builders, every homeowner can now enjoy the primal pleasures of fire without breaking local fire codes, or the bank.

A vast array of ideas for incorporating fire features into your backyard landscape have been compiled for this book. Product manufacturers, architects, landscape and interior designers, custom home and pool builders, artists, and others are all represented here. From portable fire features you can purchase and install yourself, to permanent backyard fixtures designed and built by professionals, there is something to inspire everyone within these pages.

Flush mounted in the deck, a double row of ring and fire puts on an impressive show. *Courtesy of Travis Industries*

CHIMENEAS & FIRE PITS

Chimeneas are front-loading, portable fireplaces with a bulging body and vertical chimney. With origins in Mexico, chimeneas are traditionally made from clay and were originally used indoors for heating and cooking. Today, chimeneas have become a popular feature for outdoor entertaining. While those in the Southwest may enjoy the more traditional clay versions, they are now made in a range of more durable materials suitable for use in cooler and wetter climes. Low cost and easy portability make chimeneas a viable option for homeowners who would like to extend their outdoor entertaining into the cooler months of spring and autumn without spending a lot of money. While most chimeneas on the market require wood for fuel, there are some gas-powered models available as well. Chimeneas can be used on patios, on the lawn, and even on wooden decks. If you do plan on using a chimenea on a wooden deck, it's a good idea to purchase a fireproof mat first.

A chimenea stands guard over a petite spa-side patio. The tile effect was created in cast and stenciled concrete using color hardeners.
Courtesy of XcelDeck™

Fire pits are another budget-friendly option for homeowners who dream of sitting outdoors around the glow of a fire with friends. Most fire pits are simple, inground constructions made from bricks, concrete, or stone. The more ambitious do-it-yourselfer is fully capable of building a fire pit in the backyard, with materials available at local home improvement stores. For those who would like to install a fire pit in a pre-existing patio or deck, the project may be a little more difficult, requiring the help of a professional.

Rough stacked stone forms a base for a gas fire pit, easily lit and as quickly shut off when these homeowners head off to bed. *Courtesy of Joe Murray Landscapes*

A cowboy takes center stage when the fire pit's not lit. Boulders are a natural fit for the seating, with a large safety zone of pea gravel for this pm gathering site.
Courtesy of Gym & Swim

This aluminum and stainless steel Luminarium™ is Asian-inspired and lights up with the turn of a switch. *Courtesy of Fire Designs, Inc./Moberg Fireplaces*

This fire pit beckons a couple to share intimate seating, a glass of wine, and the fire's warmth and glow. *Courtesy of Anchor Block Company*

Top right:
Tucked away in a corner of the yard, a pair of hammocks calls. The surrounding foliage creates the illusion of a backyard getaway, complete with comforting fire bowl for after-work escapes. *Courtesy of Dan Berger, LandPlan Landscaping*

Bottom right:
Nothing is set in stone, except for this fire pit that is. A cover keeps rain from collecting there. *Courtesy of Classic Garden Design, LLC*

Far right:
Flames fed by natural gas or propane have been framed by an artful bowl, perfect for encircling with chairs. The advantage of this fire, whether piped from a pre-existing line or a storage tank, is a smoke and ember-free atmosphere. *Courtesy of Colombo Construction Corp.*

Left:
A fire bowl combines with nature in a quest to draw men out into the elements. *Courtesy of Colombo Construction Corp.*

Above:
A pergola and much-loved privacy screen define a patio space designed as an additional room. *Photo by Kim Kurian/Courtesy of Greenridge Landscaping*

Left:
A sculptural chimenea sheds heat and adds a focal point to a wooden deck. *Courtesy of Empire Comfort Systems, Inc.*

Below:
Fire and water: Each offers comfort and here they sit side by side on a flagstone patio. *Courtesy of Artistic Pools, Inc.*

Right:
A small flame in the center of the table lights up serene summer nights with the flip of a switch. *Courtesy of O.W. Lee, Inc.*

Below:
A fire bowl doubles as table in this interesting upgrade on the fire pit. *Courtesy of O.W. Lee, Inc.*

Top right:
A fire pit sits dead center in a circular patio, overlooked by planters and a bench. *Courtesy of Barkman Concrete*

Bottom right:
This octagonal fire pit has a built-in bench providing convenient seating for those seeking warmth. *Courtesy of Pavestone Company*

Far right:
A fire pit with surrounding built-in seating forms a central attraction in a patio designed with entertaining in mind. *Courtesy of Superlite Block, Inc.*

A fountain inside the bowl creates an interesting visual effect combining the two seemingly unmixable elements of fire and water. *Courtesy of Travis Industries*

Above:
Above a swimming pool and sundeck, three octagonal pits were established for fire, water, and a garden mix. *Courtesy of TimberTech*

Left:
A fire basket filled with "stones" fills a break in a balcony balustrade. These stones flicker to life via gas at the touch of a switch. *Courtesy of Scott Zucker*

Right:

Here an outdoor fireplace combines the features of a fireplace, a grill, and a piece of sculpture. A series of racks can be fitted above the firebox for grilling and the fireplace's unique shape and construction help it to double as a piece of garden sculpture. *Courtesy of Rais & Wittus, Inc.*

Below:

A low stone wall built around this fire pit serves as a bench, far away enough to avoid smoke and sparks, but close enough to reach with a marshmallow stick. *Courtesy of Conte & Conte, LLC*

PATIO GEMS

A fireplace on the patio serves multiple purposes. Besides acting as a gathering spot where cool evenings last long past sundown, a fireplace on the patio can be an aesthetic point of interest, the culminating visual feature in the backyard theater. Or perhaps it's merely one component of an entire outdoor living area – transplanting interior creature comforts into the fresh air. The flicker of flames under wide-open skies is a dream even the landless urbanite can fulfill, with gas-powered fireplaces designed specifically for outdoor use. This chapter contains an array of fireplace designs. From towering wood-powered masonry constructions clad in stone, to fireplaces built in the form of their interior counterparts, you'll see a mix of materials, styles, and functions sure to inspire your own backyard gem.

Arms spread, this fireplace appears almost maternal in its welcoming embrace.
Courtesy of Harrison Design Associates

This patio center was created in the south-western style that is characteristic of its surroundings in the mountains west of Denver, Colorado. A trellis of Douglas fir harmonizes with evergreens growing around the house. The freedom of stucco construction allows the kiva fireplace to rise in artfully curvaceous lines, a bright white element in a palette of natural hues. *Courtesy of Peter Budeiri + Associates, Architects*

A wide sweep of stone and impressive open hearth size create a sense of ceremony for this raised, circular patio. The lighting is subtly enhanced with sidelights and built-ins on the steps and hearth wall. *Courtesy of Jeffrey D. Sessler, Blue Water Pools & Spas*

Left:
A mantel lends an atmosphere of home to an outdoor fireplace, and side woodbins double as display shelves. *Courtesy of MarcoDesigns*

Bottom left:
Whitewashed bricks in a ready to order fireplace compliment the slate flagstones on the patio. Cast iron tools help keep the firebox clean and a metal cap on the chimney keeps it free of debris. *Courtesy of Laneventure*

Above:
A ready for delivery fireplace graces this lawn area, an attractive and quick fix to today's desire for indoor amenities outside.
Courtesy of Laneventure

Right:
Simulating a mountain stream, water collects in an aboveground spa and travels down two waterfalls into the pool. Flagstones around the pool and the fireplace in the background create a very solid, natural looking space. *Courtesy of Luciole Design*

Tile adds accent to a fireplace, in fitting with this perfect Florida environment. *Courtesy of McGarvey Custom Homes*

A stone fireplace dominates a raised patio, adding incentive to linger on this commanding plateau. *Courtesy of Artistic Pools, Inc.*

This fireplace was made from fire resistant concrete blocks then covered with stucco to give it a more decorative appearance. This combination of materials is commonly used in the construction of outdoor fireplaces. *Courtesy of Inside Out*

Left:
Palm leaves on the upholstery give a lighter, slightly tropical air to the dignity and ambiance of this outdoor living room. Red candles make a terrific accent against the primarily dark colors. *Courtesy of Gib-San Pools, Ltd.*

Bottom left:
A monstrous retaining wall gains ornament from an equally impressive fireplace and chimney. *Courtesy of Harrison Design Associates*

Outdoor dining becomes elegant in this setting. Guests are treated to a sight and sound environment with this simply fabulous fireplace. It certainly celebrates the interaction of water, fire, earth, and air. *Courtesy of Geremia Pools, Inc.*

A ventilated hood caps a gorgeous stucco center-piece, complete with a built-in wood box, hearth, mantel, and chimney to chase away any evening chill. *Courtesy of Orco Concrete Block Co.*

Just as the fireplace and mantel function in the living room, dramatic architectural elements are achieved outdoors as well. *Courtesy of Cultured Stone® Corporation*

Yellow, orange, and turquoise give this backyard setting a distinctly Southwestern feel. Beneath the trellis, an outdoor bar provides a lofty congregation space, while cushioned chairs circle up to the fire. *Courtesy of Dan Berger, LandPlan Landscaping*

An intimate patio creates a couple's retreat by this massive stucco fireplace, overhung by wooden trellis. *Courtesy of Terra Designs*

A fireplace constructed of the same bricks as the house creates a seamless transition from indoors to out. Its presence transforms a landing into destination, a room just beyond the indoors. *Courtesy of Brick SouthEast, Inc.*

Top:

An outdoor boardroom of sorts, this special meeting site was furnished with two rows of wooden rocking chairs lined up before a massive stone fireplace. The rustic effect and country setting create a relaxed atmosphere where guests tend to linger. *Courtesy of Design Studios West, Inc.*

Bottom:

An outdoor "living room suite" in wicker clusters beside an outdoor fireplace. The color and the pattern of the cushions complement the brushed concrete patio. *Courtesy of Winston Furniture*

Medieval architecture meets modern function in a brilliant mix of old and new. A twenty-foot tall torreon ("tower" in Spanish) commands a spectacular view of the surrounding scrubland. The structure was made from moss rock and features a stone fireplace built into the structure of the tower. *Courtesy of Duty & Germanas Architects, Inc.*

A wood fire burns cheerfully in the hearth of this outdoor fireplace. To protect people sitting nearby from sparks, a mesh screen can be pulled across the hearth. *Courtesy of Desa Heating Products*

Right:

These homeowners wanted it all. The perimeter of their deck includes a grill station, a fireplace, and a fire-pit – so no one is ever left out of the light on a cool night. *Courtesy of Heatilator*

Below:

Festive blue and gold tiles decorate the edges of this fireplace's firebox. The tiles on the fireplace along with several other elements such as a terra cotta tiled mantel and hearth and a wooden trellis reveal a Southwestern influence on the outdoor room's design. *Courtesy of Fogazzo Wood Fired Ovens and Barbecues*

A large fireplace flanked by classic pergolas stand poolside. After a late day of swimming, bathers can climb out of the pool and dry themselves off in front of a fire. *Courtesy of MarcoDesigns and Lasting Impressions*

Top left:
An outdoor fireplace is the centerpiece of a focal brick wall. Evening gatherings are illuminated by the fire's warm glow, as well as sconces on the corner posts. *Courtesy of I-XL Industries, Ltd.*

Bottom left:
A lot of zones, tied together with circular shapes, were fashioned for this backyard environment. In the foreground, an intimate seating area was defined by a circular patio. In the far distance, a fireplace beckons after sunset. *Courtesy of O.W. Lee, Inc.*

In this stunning take on a living room outdoors, family members watch television fireside, backed by the pool's two walls of cascading water. *Courtesy of Toll Brothers*

A leering gargoyle and a pair of stone lions add character to the presence of a brick fireplace in grand Edwardian style. A wood-fired oven and fireplace transfer some of the grandeur and comfort of an old manor house to an outdoor setting. *Courtesy of Brick SouthEast, Inc.*

Stonework creates storybook charm for this outdoor fireplace and wood fired oven. *Courtesy of Conte & Conte, LLC*

Top left:
Woodbins help keep wood dry and close at hand. *Courtesy of MarcoDesigns*

Bottom left:
Massive wooden beams form the bare bones of a roof, offering a sense of shelter without detracting from the open-air experience. Below, wicker chairs sidle up to a stucco fireplace. *Courtesy of Scott Zucker*

Traces of the desert beyond were brought into this courtyard. Cacti and other desert plants live along the outer edge of the courtyard and water features hidden in artificial rocks create fountains that mimic the peaceful gurgle of natural springs. *Courtesy of Toll Brothers*

Top left:
A stucco fireplace anchors one corner of a wall encircling this desert oasis. *Courtesy of Patio Pools of Tucson, Inc.*

Left:
A grey brick fireplace built into a surrounding wall provides privacy and warmth for bathers. Boulders create a natural border for a built-in pool. *Courtesy of Patio Pools of Tucson*

Above:
A sunken patio circles up to the fire, contained in a three-tiered stone chimney with an expansive arched firebox. *Courtesy of Environmental Landscape Associates*

Right:
A flash of flaming color needs no kindling in this outdoor hearth. Instead, a clever conversion turned this patio still-life into a healthy goldfish pond, complete with the sound of falling water. *Courtesy of Dan Berger, LandPlan Landscaping*

A concrete bridge reaches across a serene swimming pool to a patio where a gas-powered fireplace lights a dramatic length of wall. *Courtesy of Ibarra Rosano Design Architects*

A raised patio and fireplace create a destination point in the yard.
Courtesy of Gym & Swim

Left:
A wooden trellis overhead provides a small measure of shade, keeping off the worst of the summer sun while still letting some light and heat in. Beyond the shade, the cool blue waters of the swimming pool beckon invitingly. *Courtesy of MarcoDesigns*

Below:
A stone fireplace is the crown jewel in an environment rich in beautiful stone masonry. The pool skirting and bases for the pool-house pillars are two more ways the environment was tied together. *Courtesy of Artistic Pools*

PAVILIONS &
DEDICATED STRUCTURES

While some homeowners choose to leave their outdoor fireplaces and kitchens out in the open and exposed to all the elements that nature has to offer, others opt to include some kind of structural component in the design of their outdoor environment. A pergola or arbor offers shade in the afternoon heat and a sense of security at night. Most often found in close range to an area directly adjacent to the home, these structures are easy to construct and can even be purchased from a local home design store or lumberyard. Moving away from the house and into the wilds of the backyard, a pavilion offers even greater architectural presence, more protection from the sun, and shelter from the rain. A roof overhead may limit skyward views, but a lack of walls still allows cool evening breezes to pass through.

Right:
Sturdy columns of stacked stone anchor this outdoor pavilion, furnished with a cook station and ready to provide shade and shelter spa-side. *Courtesy of Shasta Pools & Spas*

Right:
A backyard pavilion features a fireplace dead center to warm both dining and cook areas. *Courtesy of Gib-San Pools, Ltd.*

Below:
A sweet stucco structure provides shelter poolside. *Courtesy of Gib-San Pools, Ltd.*

Top:
The setting sun colors the sky above a white large tiled patio. An attached pavilion overhangs the cooking area that sits poolside. *Courtesy of Shasta Pools & Spas*

Bottom left & right:
The interior of this pavilion is richly furnished with comfortable wicker chairs and a fireplace. A roof helps keep both the sun and the rain off the interior, while open sides allow air to circulate freely. *Courtesy of Luciole Design*

Not for the casual outdoor cook, this outdoor kitchen is equipped with a grill, a range, and a wood-fired oven. Outdoor chefs can prepare anything from steaks on the grill to pizza baked in the oven. A leaping dolphin leads the way towards the pool, though guests are advised to wait an hour before enjoying that part of the room. *Courtesy of Karen Black's Kitchens and Rooms by Design*

A sturdy trellis and stucco wall add room-like structure to a space dominated by a functional hearth. *Courtesy of Tropitone*

Above:
At the far edge of the patio, a pergola-covered lounging area is shaded by palm trees in the afternoon and lit by the flicker of flames at night. *Courtesy of McGarvey Custom Homes*

Left:
A colossal fireplace and arbor flank a built-in pool, adding an impressive backdrop and a desirable destination on the other side. *Courtesy of Madison Swimming Pool Co., Inc.*

Above:
This grand patio is defined by columns and topped with beams and the sky above. A roaring fire beckons on a cool night. *Courtesy of DL Ackerman Design Group*

Left:
Applied woodwork on a stucco surround makes for a beautiful frame around this outdoor fireplace. The rustic setting, atop bricks and backed by an ivy-covered wall, is the perfect complement to a sheltered seating area. *Courtesy of Martin Hearth & Heating*

Right:
A stone chimney anchors the open beams of an outdoor room. *Courtesy of Harrison Design Associates*

Below:
An expansive pergola crowns a patio/fireplace area set amidst an expanse of lawn. *Courtesy of Trellis Structures*

Stone masonry unites a wonderful semi-circular backyard kitchen. The wood-fired oven stands as centerpiece, the chairs circled around an island stage. *Courtesy of Los Angeles Ovenworks*

Right:
A smooth stucco fireplace forms the centerpiece for a beautiful pergola room, comfortably furnished for indoor-style living in the open air. *Courtesy of Inside Out*

Bottom right:
A backyard slope is used for rocks and cascading water running into the spa and pool below. The poolside pavilion has a fireplace for warmth and an overhead fan when nature lacks a breeze. Grill, fridge, and sink make for an outdoor kitchen. *Courtesy of Mission Pools*

A trellis structure crowns mellow yellow walls, offering a sense of security and architectural interest to this outdoor living area. *Courtesy of Kelly Melendez, MAK Studio*

Top:
A covered pavilion shelters indoor-quality furnishings from unfavorable weather conditions, taking luxury to a new outdoor level. *Courtesy of Travis Industries*

Bottom:
An arbor and patio extend peninsula-like into the pool. Moonlit dinner parties and night-time swimmers are warmed next to the towering stone chimney. *Courtesy of Aqua Blue Pools*

AT THE EDGE OF THE EAVES

In warmer, southern climates, a typical roof extends beyond the edge of the house to shelter a frequently-used patio. While these geographic regions experience a longer, hotter summer season, the shelter provided during cooler winter evenings is made more inhabitable, and enjoyable, by the decadence of a glowing fire. Many of the spaces shown in this chapter are complete outdoor environments, where the activity of the house has been moved to the outdoors. Nature-loving

Fire and water are irresistible lures on this back porch with a magnificent bay view. *Courtesy of Telescope Casual Furniture, Inc.*

northerners can also find respite from drab indoor living out on the porch, where fireplaces are being included in new home designs and added during remodeling projects to extend the living space of the home to the outdoors. The flourish of gas-powered fireplaces on the market has made including a fireplace at the edge of the eaves an easy option for homeowners.

Wicker furnishings designed by Eddie Bauer provide a deeply relaxing space next to this roaring outdoor fire. From the same collection, a dining room set includes chairs rugged enough for outdoors, but comfy enough that guests tend to linger long after desert. *Courtesy of Laneventure*

Smooth grey surfaces provide a contemporary feel to this outdoor fire setting, and keep maintenance at a minimum. *Courtesy of Gym & Swim*

Above:
A two-way fireplace sheds warmth under an overhang and further out on the balcony. Wide hearth ledges provide seating on either side on crisp evenings. *Courtesy of Cultured Stone® Corporation*

Top right:
A big brick fireplace emphasizes the luxury of height in the ceiling created for this summery outdoor room. *Courtesy of Harrison Design Associates*

Bottom right:
This patio is well equipped with a brick oven, a fireplace giving warmth on chilly nights, a wet sink, and electrical outlets for television or stereo equipment. *Courtesy of I-XL Industries, Ltd.*

Left:
After splashing around in the pool, guests can emerge dripping wet and dry off in front of the fire. The entire area is sheltered from mosquitoes by screen netting. *Courtesy of Harbourside Custom Homes*

Below:
A glimpse of outdoor living at its finest: elegant marble floors, plush furniture, and wax candles in the fireplace give this outdoor living room an atmosphere of elegance and sophistication. *Courtesy of McGarvey Custom Homes*

Right:

A brick half wall provides a private space where guests can change into or out of bathing suits on one side. On the other, a roaring fire is the centerpiece of a sheltered gathering area. *Courtesy of Rais & Wittus, Inc.*

Below:

A half wall between lanai and the outdoors creates a focal point, illuminated by a ventless gas fireplace. *Courtesy of McGarvey Custom Homes*

Dark upholstery, a carpet, and plenty of pillows make curling up in this patio room an enticing proposal. *Courtesy of Harrison Design Associates*

Built over an existing patio, this pavilion houses a living room and a dining room as well as a kitchenette equipped with a prep sink and a barbeque grill. A stone fireplace provides both heating and atmosphere. *Courtesy of Harrison Design Associates*

ADDITIONS TO THE ARCHITECTURE

Taking advantage of existing chimneys and architecture, some homeowners include an outdoor fireplace within the structure of the house. Built into walls or butting up to an interior fireplace, these designs may be masonry constructions or manufactured, gas-powered hearth products, depending on the homeowner's preference and budget. For people adding on to their homes, an outdoor fireplace may be a secondary consideration, but becomes a valuable bonus that doesn't have to tack on a lot of cost to a renovation project. Such close-to-home constructions are desirable because they take advantage of existing electrical outlets and provide a convenient location for entertaining. Whether building anew or adjusting what's already there, fireplaces added on to the home's architecture provide yet another option for incorporating fire into an outdoor living space.

Above & right:
A winding path meanders through the flowerbeds, leading up to this outdoor room. Guests can sit comfortably next to the fireplace in this porch safely out of the sun and rain. The porch front is open so as not to obscure the view of the gardens behind the house. *Courtesy of Fitzgibbons Design*

Right:
A fireplace is a central focal point in a walkout-basement room, separated from the elements by crisp white drapes.
Courtesy of Harrison Design Associates

Below:
A pavilion-like structure was added on to this home to create an outdoor gathering spot for sunbathers. A fireplace extends its use into the fall and early spring months.
Courtesy of Gib-San Pools, Ltd.

A stone grotto tucked under a deck creates a cool and alluring retreat in the heat of the summer. Bench seating around a roaring waterfall proves irresistible.
Courtesy of Harrison Design Associates

A wall of Cultured Stone®
creates a privacy barrier and a
safe spot for a warm fire on this
open porch. *Courtesy of
Cultured Stone® Corporation*

The addition of an exterior chimney and porch were a natural fit for this balanced home clad in board and batten. A metal frame around this firebox contrasts pleasingly with the board formed concrete. *Courtesy of Rex Hohlbein Architects*

A sliver of deck skirts the home and courtyard, evocative of Japanese design. The concrete of pavers and towering chimney create contrast with the natural wood and foliage tones that frame them. *Courtesy of Rex Hohlbein Architects*

Above:
A raised firebox makes tending the flames easier, as this thoughtful design – complete with ledges to facilitate repose – illustrates. *Courtesy of Rex Hohlbein Architects*

Top right and right:
A chimney doubles for both indoor and outdoor fires, and turns a side-yard into a tempting gathering spot on summer evenings. *Courtesy of Rossetti Perchik Architecture*

A brick doorway ushers one to a wooden deck and frames a solitary bench sitting against the far railing. Beyond, a hammock promises respite. A fireplace was installed to permit use of the patio in the fall and winter months. *Courtesy of David F. Schultz Associates, Ltd.*

Top:
An enormous fireplace and its towering chimney create a focal point for this inviting courtyard.
Courtesy of Toll Brothers

Bottom:
In recent years, entryway courtyards have begun to replace porches as the gathering place and point
of welcome for the house. As a result they often have design features such as ornamental waterfalls
and fountains, and more practical touches like an outdoor fireplace. *Courtesy of Toll Brothers*

Opposite a rounded fireplace, an ornamental waterfall offers a tranquil counterpart to the crackle of flames. *Courtesy of Toll Brothers*

A see-through fireplace sheds its glow on indoors and out within the open wall of a lanai. *Courtesy of McGarvey Custom Homes*

Top left:
Glass pocket doors slide away, eliminating the barrier between this living room and the loggia. *Courtesy of KAA Design Group*

Bottom left:
This see-through firebox was installed in such a way that the flames can be enjoyed from the back porch or the family room within. *Courtesy of Hearthstone, Inc.*

After the sun has set and the light begins to fade, an outdoor fireplace becomes the ideal place to congregate. This back porch is the perfect place to sit and watch the stars come out. *Courtesy of Hearthstone Homes, Inc.*

Right:
A stone coffee table is the stable center around which the rest of this outdoor room has come together. Subtle earth tones keep the manner of the room calm, while patterns on the upholstery help stimulate visual interest. *Courtesy of Harbourside Custom Homes*

Bottom right:
Thick cushions and extra-wide chairs offer an invitation to curl up in front of this stainless steel fireplace. The simple lines of contemporary architecture minimize distractions, keeping the focus on relaxation. *Courtesy of Gloster Furniture, Inc.*

A towering chimney and tiled roof were added to this home, capturing its Spanish Colonial feel while creating a new outdoor area for living and entertaining. *Courtesy of David Gast & Associates*

Above:
Upholstered chairs like these make comfortable places to sit, whether or not there's a fire in the fireplace. Wrought iron candleholders and a dried flower wreath along with the wicker chairs give the area around the fireplace a very comfortable, country feel. *Courtesy of Brick SouthEast, Inc.*

Top left:
Pillared arches open a room up to the outside world. *Courtesy of Harrison Design Associates*

Left:
Sling-style seating and an adjustable umbrella add creature comforts to this patio setting by day. By night, ferns move aside for a roaring fire to warm the area's occupants. *Courtesy of Winston Furniture*

Far left:
This outdoor fireplace was a natural addition when the homeowners elected to add stone veneer to their home's exterior. *Courtesy of El Dorado Stone*

Above:
Just as the fireplace and mantel function in the living room, dramatic architectural elements are achieved outdoors as well. *Courtesy of Cultured Stone® Corporation*

Top right:
A fire blazes merrily in the hearth of this outdoor fireplace. A niche beneath the hearth stores wood and keeps it dry. Pink stucco around the hearth and the chimney matches the shingles on the house's roof. *Courtesy of Fogazzo Wood Fired Ovens and Barbecues*

Right:
Acanthus leaves and rosebuds decorate the surround on this outdoor fireplace. Classic designs that would be at home on an indoor fireplace are equally at home outdoors. *Courtesy of Harrison Design Associates*

Top left:
A pavilion-like structure was added on to this home to create an outdoor gathering spot for bathers. A fireplace extends its use into the fall and early spring months. *Courtesy of Gib-San Pools, Ltd.*

Top right:
An outdoor cook center is handsomely framed in stone. *Courtesy of Semco Distributing, Inc.*

Left:
Two dancing sculptures top fountains that draw the eye to an outdoor fireplace and towering chimney, together working to create a dramatic site line in this patio environment. *Courtesy of Oslund and Associates*

Right:
Ascending display shelves, as well as seating and sidewalls, show off the masonry work lavished on this wonderful backyard entrance. *Courtesy of Semco Distributing, Inc.*

Bottom right:
Stacked stone was used generously to frame a flagstone patio, with a seating wall and fireplace defining the comfort of this hardscape material. *Courtesy of Brian Higley, Land-scape Architect / Architecture by Peter Sweeny, Architect*

Left:
Gas fires can actually save on fuel costs for the suburban home-owner. They burn clean and are very low maintenance. *Courtesy of Lennox Hearth Products*

Bottom left:
A sliding metal door. connects the interior of the house with a courtyard. *Courtesy of Ibarra Rosano Design Architects*

Bottom right:
An outdoor fireplace adds heat to cobalt blue walls. *Courtesy of Ibarra Rosano Design Architects*

The re-design of a backyard space adjacent to a modernist house included a pergola and privacy screens, as well as the use of a pre-existing chimney for the new outdoor fireplace. *Courtesy of Shipley Architects*

Left:
Wooden architectural details soften the effect of this modernist home's concrete exterior. The utility of a chimney is doubled by the inclusion of an exterior fireplace.
Courtesy of Rex Hohlbein Architects

Below:
A brick pool house offers a sense of Colonial scale in its fireside retreat.
Courtesy of Harrison Design Associates

Right:
A fireplace is a central feature in a brick-clad outdoor room. *Courtesy of Harrison Design Associates*

Bottom right:
Old world ambience in the form of thick stone pillars, sturdy wood beams, and ageless furnishings characterize an expansive room open along one wall to the outdoors. *Courtesy of Thomas Bartlett Interiors. Photography by Matthew Millman*

WOOD FIRED OVENS

Wood fired ovens have been used for centuries, but this ancient technology is enjoying a resurgence of popularity with the current focus on the home's outdoor environments. While wood fired ovens are certainly an option indoors, people are choosing to include them outside on the patio, where smoke drifts away with the breeze. Typically constructed around a pre-fabricated masonry box, wood fired ovens provide temperatures far above those of normal ovens, and can bake a crispy pizza in just minutes. These constructions can cook a lot more than just pizza, though. The taste of meats and vegetables benefit from the flavor of wood smoke, and cooking becomes an adventurous, unpredictable, and altogether delectable experience with the use of a wood fired oven. The glow and warmth of the oven can be enjoyed long after dinner has been served, doubling as a fireplace once its rcal work is done.

Reclaimed oak wine barrel staves are used to fire a pizza oven. Once ready, the fire is swept to the side, the surface mopped with a wet rag, and the pizza inserted for a quick bake that could take as few as three minutes. *Courtesy of Peter A. Zepponi, AIA Architects*

Top:
Side tables add convenience for the chef who is busy tending flames, shaping rising dough, and shifting wood and loaves about the confines of a pretty wood-fired stove.
Courtesy of Alchymia Wood Fired Ovens

Middle:
Sculpted concrete – from the patio surfacing and seating, to the spiraling garlic tower of a wood-fired oven – creates an organic atmosphere in this tropical backyard retreat.
Courtesy of Alchymia Wood Fired Ovens

Bottom:
An onion-domed oven attractively houses its kindling below, the small cook-space above.
Courtesy of Alchymia Wood Fired Ovens

The phoenix is a mythological bird often associated with heat and fire. Here a wood-fired oven has been sculpted to look like a phoenix with its body being the main part of the oven and its wings curling to nestle a pair of benches. *Courtesy of Kiko Denzer*

A wood-fired oven has been sculpted from clay, sand, and straw to resemble a frog. Decorative as well as functional, this oven doubles as a garden sculpture when not in use. The artist, Kiko Denzer, also teaches and writes manuals on using earth to make ovens, art, and architectural sculpture. *Courtesy of Kiko Denzer*

Top left:
Here's an ironic twist. Instead of the turkey being inside the oven, the oven is inside the turkey. *Courtesy of Kiko Denzer*

Top right:
The nautilus shape of a snail's shell lends itself quite well to the exterior shape of a wood-fired oven. *Courtesy of Kiko Denzer*

A Haida-inspired totemic figure looks out from beside an earthen house in Oregon. It is also a wood-fired oven which opens to the rear, and serves for baking bread and other foods. A fascinating effect, particularly on a cold day. *Courtesy of Kiko Denzer*

Head cocked, a falcon shaped wood-fired oven gazes intently at something across the patio. Decorative as well as being functional this oven is a marvelous showpiece for an outside room. An awning provides shelter and protects the oven. *Courtesy of Kiko Denzer*

Above:
A "sophisticated" wood-fired oven combines technology in the form of a cast-iron door and thermometer with the age old art of cooking pizzas and breads. *Courtesy of Los Angeles Ovenworks*

Top right:
A handsome cook center was created in stucco on this stone patio, the wood oven doubling as outdoor sculpture. *Courtesy of Los Angeles Ovenworks.*

Right:
Wood-fired ovens have a reputation for being able to reach high cooking temperatures. This is achieved because the walls, floor, and ceiling all store and radiate heat. Some ovens have been known to reach temperatures of 500 degrees Celsius (932 Farenheit) and can cook a pizza in about a minute and a half. *Courtesy of Fogazzo Wood Fired Ovens and Barbecues*

A matching barbeque grill was built next to this wood fired oven. While it is possible to cook meats in a wood-fired oven, some outdoor cooks prefer to cook meat on a grill where the meat is easier to watch and reach. *Courtesy of Fogazzo Wood Fired Ovens and Barbecues*

Wood-fired ovens can reach high temperatures very quickly and can generate a large amount of heat and smoke. If the oven is small enough and has a small enough door or a door that closes needs a chimney in order to help vent the heat and smoke. This oven has been fitted with a metal stovepipe to carry the smoke and heat away from the dining area. *Courtesy of Fogazzo Wood Fired Ovens and Barbecues*

A stainless steel range and a wood-fired oven eagerly await the next backyard barbeque. The patio is open with plenty of room for barbeque guests to meet and mingle.
Courtesy of Dan Berger, LandPlan Landscaping

Common brick painted black forms the exterior of a modernist clay wood-burning oven. A copper plate connected by a cable to a 32-pound counterweight was used as the door. *Courtesy of Shipley Architects*

Right:
The front of a wood-fired oven shelters underneath a wooden arbor. Terra cotta ornaments and a rough stucco surface give the oven a rough, old-fashioned look. Wooden lattice doors protect the contents of these cabinets from over inquisitive animals. *Courtesy of Fogozzo Wood Fired Ovens and Barbecues*

Bottom right:
Many wood-fired ovens feature a small niche underneath the oven for storing wood and keeping it dry. This particular oven features a separate compartment for storing kindling. *Courtesy of Fogazzo Wood Fired Ovens and Barbeques*

Far right:
Superior Clay Corporation manufactures products specifically designed for creating outdoor fireplaces, grills, and wood-fired ovens finished in salt-glazed bricks designed to resist Nature's worst weather. The company has instructions for building your own fireplace and wood-fired oven on its website, www.superiorclay.com. *Courtesy of Superior Clay Corporation*

COOK CENTERS

Outdoor cooking is no longer limited to an open ring of fire or a charcoal-powered grill. Entire kitchens are cropping up in backyards, where built-in grills, refrigerators, and even sinks are making their way onto the patio. All-out kitchen workstations in the open air mean meals come to life outside. Avid chefs perform their craft with ease and enjoyment in the fresh air, without going back and forth from inside to out. These outdoor cook centers provide a convenient solution to outdoor entertainment, bringing it to a whole new level.

This barbeque combines the enjoyment of cooking and eating outdoors with the atmosphere of an outdoor fire. *Courtesy of Robert H. Peterson Co. and Fire Magic*

Blue tile was used to construct the hearth, for those who want to get closer to stoke the flames. To the left, a small brick oven is used by the family baker. *Courtesy of I-XL Industries, Ltd*

An adobe wood-fired oven, built-in grill, poolside bar, spa, and distinctive slide are made even more magical by the appearance of a rainbow. No detail was forgotten in the design of this backyard desert retreat, where outdoor meals are marked by fresh air and open views. *Courtesy of Patio Pools of Tucson*

Top:
A perimeter wall forms the backdrop for an extensive backyard kitchen. Neo-classical elements like the pergola, fountain, and statuary establish an aura of elegance and upscale style. *Courtesy of Fogazzo Wood Fired Ovens and Barbecues*

Bottom:
While a rectangular oven may not heat up as quickly as a round oven, a rectangular shape offers larger dimensions inside, good for baking large amounts of bread and other baked treats. *Courtesy of Fogazzo Wood Fired Ovens and Barbecues*

This timelessly appealing environment was created with the use of rock, water, and fire. *Courtesy of Prestige Pools & Spas*

Whimsy and artistry combine in an outdoor fire center that includes an expansive hearth, a wood-fired oven set in a conical tower, and a party-sized grill. *Courtesy of Conte & Conte, LLC*

An outside wall got a makeover in concrete that was cast and tinted to replicate real stone. A built-in barbeque and fire pit provide the glow. *Courtesy of Cultured Stone® Corporation*

To keep most of the outdoor activity in one space, an outdoor fireplace and living room share the same space with a barbeque grill. This arrangement also allows the cook to socialize with his guests while grilling. *Courtesy of Gib-San Pools, Ltd.*

This outdoor room fits snug underneath the overhanging second-floor porch of this stone home. Protected from the sun and the weather, family members enjoy meals cooked on the grill, their favorite television programs, and the ambient warmth of a fireplace. *Courtesy of Bost Construction*

Stone, wood, and brick combine in this artisan-built fireplace and barbeque unit, perfect crown jewel to a patio environment of slate flagstones. *Courtesy of Conte & Conte, LLC*

Left:
Wood-fired ovens can be built in various sizes and forms. A round oven like this one heats up fairly quickly and more evenly, which makes it ideally suited for cooking pizza. Here, a pergola built atop neo-classical columns defines the outdoor kitchen and eating area. *Courtesy of Fogazzo Wood Fired Ovens and Barbecues*

Below:
An extensive outdoor kitchen features a stove, grill, refrigerator, and a warming drawer. The towering fireplace extends the season for dinner parties and outdoor gatherings. *Courtesy of Environmental Landscape Associates, Inc.*

Right:
A wood-fired oven is a central focal point of a lavish outdoor kitchen. *Courtesy of Peter A. Zepponi, AIA Architects*

Bottom right:
After a late-season dinner outside, an outdoor fireplace means not having to go inside quite so soon. *Courtesy of Travis Industries*

The fresh-air location of this kitchen allows the inclusion of a wood-fired oven. Natural stone was used for perimeter half-walls, columns, and planters. The entire outdoor area is covered by a timber frame construction that makes it a memorable outdoor destination. *Courtesy of Fogazzo Wood Fired Ovens and Barbecues*

Stucco walls, Italian ceramic countertops, and terra cotta tiles on the oven roof give this outdoor kitchen a southwestern look. Wood-fired ovens are called "hornos" in the Southwest and generally have a cone-shaped interior. *Courtesy of Fogazzo Wood Fired Ovens and Barbecues*

Tuscany is just outside the backdoor for these homeowners. A passion for food and good wine is shared among friends in the fresh air, where a fireplace keeps the temperature comfortable year-round. *Courtesy of Environmental Landscape Associates, Inc.*

RESOURCE GUIDE

Architects

Peter Budeiri + Associates, Architects
New York, New York
(212) 683-2008

Duty & Germanas Architects, Inc.
Santa Fe, New Mexico
(505) 989-8882

Fryday & Doyne Architecture
  Interior Design
Charlotte, North Carolina
(704) 372-0001
www.fryday-doyne.com

David Gast & Associates
San Francisco, California
(415) 885-2946
www.GastArchitects.com

Harrison Design Associates
Atlanta, Georgia
(404) 365-7760
www.harrisondesignassociates.com

Rex Hohlbein Architects
Bothell, Washington
(425) 487-3655
www.rexhohlbeinarchitects.com

Ibarra Rosano Design Architects
Tucson, Arizona
(520) 795-5477
www.ibarrarosano.com

KAA Design Group
Los Angeles, California
(310) 821-1400
www.kaadesigngroup.com

MAK Studio
San Francisco, California
(415) 861-5646
www.makstudio.net

Rossetti Perchik Architecture
East Hampton, New York
(631) 324-6250
www.rpaia.com

David F. Schultz Associates, Ltd.
Barrington, Illinois
(847) 381-8808
www.dfsal.com

Shipley Architects
Dallas, Texas
(214) 823-2080
www.shipleyarchitects.com

Peter A. Zepponi, AIA Architects
San Francisco, California
(415) 334-2868
www.zepponi-architects.com

Artists

Kiko Denzer
Blodgett, Oregon
(541) 438-4300
www.intabas.com/kikodenzer.html

Builders

Bost Construction
Cary, North Carolina
(919) 460-1983
www.bosthomes.com

Harbourside Custom Homes
Bonita Springs, Florida
(239) 949-0200
www.harboursidecustomhomes.com

Hearthstone Homes, Inc.
Dandridge, Tennessee
(800) 247-4442
www.hearthstonehomes.com

Home Project
Rome, Italy
valdo@homeprojectroma.com
www.homeprojectroma.com

McGarvey Custom Homes
Bonita Springs, Florida
(239) 992-8940
www.mcgarveycustomhomes.com

Toll Brothers
North America
(800) 289-8655
www.tollbrothers.com

Interior Design

DL Ackerman Design Group
El Dorado Hills, California
(916) 939-0252

Karen Black's Kitchens and Rooms
by Design
Oklahoma City, Oklahoma
(405) 858-8333
www.karenblackskitchens.com

Thomas Bartlett Interiors
Napa, California
(707) 250-1234
www.thomasbartlettinteriors.com

Landscape Design

Dan Berger, Landscape Designer
LandPlan Landscaping
Pleasanton, California
(925) 846-1989
www.landplanlandscaping.com

Classic Garden Design, LLC
Weston, Connecticut
(203) 226-2886
www.classicgardendesign.com

Conte & Conte, LLC
Greenwich, Connecticut
(203) 869-1400
www.conteandconte.com

Design Studios West, Inc.
Denver, Colorado
(303) 623-3465
www.designstudioswest.com

Environmental Landscape Associates, Inc.
Doylestown, Pennsylvania
(800) 352-9252
www.elaontheweb.com

Fitzgibbons Design
Bay Village, Ohio
(440) 899-8180

Greenridge Landscaping
Carbondale, Illinois
(618) 549-6165

Brian Higley, Landscape Architect
Beacon, New York
(845) 831-1044
www.brianhigley.com

Inside Out
Davis, California
(530) 753-7147
www.insideoutjoni.biz

Luciole Design
Sacramento, California
(916) 972-1809
www.lucioledesign.com

MarcoDesigns
Novato, California
(415) 898-5150

Joe Murray Landscapes
Tucson, Arizona
(520) 405-7478

Oslund and Associates
Minneapolis, Minnesota
(612) 359-9144
www.oaala.com

Terra Designs
Tucson, Arizona
(520) 881-4190

Zucker Design Associates
Laguna Niguel, California
(714) 478-0565
www.zuckerdesign.net

Manufacturers

Alchymia Wood Fired Ovens
Kaitaia, New Zealand
+64 09 406-1903
www.alchymia.co.nz/index.htm

Anchor Block Company
North St. Paul, Minnesota
(651) 777-8321
www.anchorblock.com

Borgert Products, Inc.
North America
www.borgertproducts.com

Barkman Concrete Ltd.
Winnipeg, Canada
(204) 667-3310
www.barkmanconcrete.com

Brick SouthEast, Inc.
Charlotte, North Carolina
(800) 622-7425
www.gobricksoutheast.com

Colombo Construction Corp.
New York, New York
(212) 343-5069
www.firefeatures.com

Cultured Stone® Corporation
Napa, California
(800) 255-1727
www.culturedstone.com

Desa Heating Products
(866) 672-6040
www.desaint.com

El Dorado Stone
North America
(760) 213-5686
www.eldoradostone.com

Empire Comfort Systems®, Inc.
Belleville, Illinois
(800) 851-3153
www.empirecomfort.com

Fire Designs, Inc./Moberg Fireplaces
Portland, Oregon
(503) 227-0547
www.firespaces.com

Fogazzo Wood Fired Ovens and
Barbecues, LLC
Arcadia, California
(866) FOGAZZO (toll free)
www.fogazzo.com

Gloster Furniture, Inc.
South Boston, Virginia
(888) GLOSTER
www.gloster.com

HearthStone Wood &
Gas Fired Stoves
North America
www.hearthstonestoves.com

Heatilator
North America
(800) 927-6841
www.heatilator.com

I-XL Masonry Supplies, Ltd.
Medicine Hat, Alberta, Canada
(403) 502-1486
www.ixlgroup.com

Laneventure
Conover, North Carolina
(800) 235-3588
www.laneventure.com

Lennox Hearth Products
Orange, California
(800) 9-LENNOX
www.lennoxhearthproducts.com

Los Angeles Ovenworks
Los Angeles, California
(323) 226-1296
www.losangelesovenworks.com

Martin Hearth & Heating
Paris, Kentucky
(866) 410-3810
www.martinhearthandheating.com

Monessen Hearth Systems
Paris, Kentucky
(866) 410-3786
www.monessenhearth.com

O.W. Lee, Inc.
Ontario, Canada
(800) 776-9533
www.owlee.com

Orco Block Company, Inc.
Stanton, California
(800) 473-6726
www.orco.com

Pavestone Company
Dallas, Texas
(972) 404-0400
www.pavestone.com

Robert H. Peterson Co./Fire Magic
City of Industry, California
(626) 369-5085
www.rhpeterson.com

Rais & Wittus, Inc.
Pound Ridge, New York
(914) 764-5679
www.wittus.com

Semco Distributing, Inc.
Perryville, Missouri
(800) 814-1072
www.semcodist.com

Superior Clay Corporation
Uhrichsville, Ohio
(740) 922-4122
www.superiorclay.com

Superlite Block
Phoenix, Arizona
(800) 366-7877
www.superliteblock.com

Telescope Casual Furniture, Inc.
Granville, New York
(518) 642-1100
www.telescopecasual.com

TimberTech
Wilmington, Ohio
(937) 655-5222
www.timbertech.com

Travis Industries
Mukilteo, Washington
(800) 654-1177
www.travisproducts.com

Trellis Structures
Beverly, Massachusetts
(888) 285-4624
www.trellisstructures.com

Tropitone Furniture Company, Inc.
Irvine, California
(949) 951-2010
www.tropitone.com

Winston Furniture
A Brown Jordan International
Company
www.winstonfurniture.com

XcelDeck™
Phoenix, Arizona
(800) 644-9131
www.xceldeck.com

Pools & Spas

Aqua Blue Pools
N. Charleston, South Carolina
(843) 767-7665
Hilton Head Island, South Carolina
(843) 379-2250
www.aquabluepools.com

Artistic Pools, Inc.
Atlanta, Georgia
(770) 458-9177
www.artisticpools.com

Blue Water Pools and Spas
Jeffrey D. Sessler
Upland, California
(909) 946-9019
www.bluewaterpoolsandspas.net

Geremia Pools, Inc.
Sacramento, California
(800) 499-7946
www.geremiapools.com

Gib-San Pools, Ltd.
Toronto, Ontario Canada
(416) 749-4361
www.GibSanPools.com

Gym & Swim
Louisville, Kentucky
(502) 426-1326
www.gymandswim.com

Madison Swimming Pool Co., Inc.
Goodlettsville, Tennessee
(615) 865-2964
www.madisonswimmingpools.com

Mission Pools
Escondido, CA 92025
(760) 743-2605
www.missionpools.com

Patio Pools of Tucson, Inc.
Tucson, Arizona
(520) 886-1211
www.patiopoolsaz.com

Prestige Pools & Spas, Inc.
Edmund, Oklahoma
(405) 340-7665
www.prestigepoolsandspasinc.com

Shasta Pools & Spas
Phoenix, Arizona
(602) 532-3750
www.shastapools.com